Bloodletting

Chloe Walker

BookLeaf Publishing

Presentation by *BookLeaf Publishing*

Web: www.bookleafpub.com

E-mail: info@bookleafpub.com

ISBN: 9789357740067

First edition 2023

For the words that carried me

To all the voices in my head

Giving me feelings

When I couldn't define my own

ACKNOWLEDGEMENT

My life was different. Beautifully unconventional. Raw and disfiguring. I grew up in a haunted house. I was raised by the 27 club, Grunge, and glamour. Gentlemen prefer blondes without holes in their heads. Morbid and obscene dead actors on a screen. Charkras mantras and graves. The Smiths, Bowie, ice cream from gas stations, Tom Petty and Hole. Zombies and vampires, Woodshops, and power tools that could disfigure.

To my father, who littered my head with the words of ghosts. Giving me spines when I couldn't find my own. For building me a world, I could be lonely in. You loved me with everything you didn't have. You gave me Warhol and Darklands. You spent a lifetime dissecting with me. Thank you for staying with me in this incarnation. You galvanized an artist for life.

For my mother, who forged me out of pain, near death, and love. I love your warrior heart and gentle nature. Your safety was encompassing, and it expanded into the cosmos that was my little world. Music was always your religion, and death was a familiar face. I chose you from the stars when I was still swimming in them. I would choose you again in every life if it meant seeing your wings.

PREFACE

All you will know of me is what you can read in black and white. My heart is hidden between the lines. I lived a life no one could see. Invisible markings carved in memory. Lines burned and etched across my face. I know we all become stories, some unwritten, some untold. One day my life will sit on a shelf. My life will become insignificant and my pilgrimage meaningless. But it's not now. I'm young. I'm free. Everything feels infinite before me. Limitless, and I can taste the stars dripping in mercury. I want to drink from the aether and let the cosmos go to my head. Swim in the void and feel eternity cradle me. I want to put everything on display like I'm a freak at a roadside attraction. Sewing together these fragments with time and the blood on my hands. I live in my thoughts. Hide in the memories permeated into my amygdala like cigarette smoke. I wonder if someone will like it. These moments in time I'm choosing to immortalize. Afraid my soul will crystallize in the light. There's so much I want to say, and so much I want to feel. Sometimes I forget that not every human heart has a baseline of crippling sensitivity. Depressed when I realize I think in an extinct language. I never saw the beauty in my isolation until now, the pain that forged my demented delicacy. I let the clot dissolve in my head. Let it pool and bubble under my skin. I'm wearing the stain. I want my hemorrhage to stain glass so time will remember I was here. And maybe one day, some of my blood will hold meaning to a stranger.

Inheritance

You left me your wings
Bloodstained and torn
They were white once
They aren't anymore
You left me your daydreams
Your demons came too
The devil whispers in my sleep
What lies did he tell you?
An obsolete language
Full of meaningless rhymes
The creative depression festering in my mind
Like the prize at the bottom of the box
How long did you suffer?
The ptsd sponsored lullabies
Shuddering at the touch
That time won't let me shake

Afflicted

Trying hard to do nothing at all
I've never felt so small
like a child left in the dark
Waiting for the light clinging to the spark
Trying to get this tar out that's stuck in my heart
Love me like I'm not tainted.
Tell me my scars are woven gold,
that I'm the kind that breaks the mold
I'm hoping that there's a part of me that hasn't
been sold
I've been traveling too long
Going nowhere as fast as I can
If I stop
I'm not sure what I will find
A piece of me that isn't marred, a bit of my soul
wrapped in scar tissue.
I'm afraid of finding a part of me that isn't
bloodied
Something clean and new
Free of stains that my demons can chew

Numb

I'm welded to the comforter
The hamper is overflowing
and there's mold in the sink
I need to brush my teeth
But I like the decay
The rot in my soft tissue
Disintegration I can control
My body feels like lead
Motivation atrophied
From the war in my head

Shadows

A stain in the family bible
Trauma never sleeps
Cemented in my hippocampus
A silent film with no end
You move mountains for them
You resent my existence
Abhor each breath
From my shredded lungs
You see your faults
In my reflection
The chasms you created
You hate that I smile
In spite of them
I love you unconditionally
In a way you withhold from me
Jealous of me
Blooming from the darkness I was born to

Rage

This feeling is new
Red in my peripheral
a foreign muscle
I'm beginning to stretch
Chasms beneath me
I can't tell above from below
Coated in crimson
I want to scream
so loud it rattles the stars
waking the Gods from their sleep
Gouge their eyes
and feel the blood trickle
down my palms
sticky and sweet
Take something from them
to make up for what you took from me

Accepted

Now that you're older
You wonder why mother never told you
How beauty leaves you unclean
And the damage that it breeds
When I was younger I dreamt my body would
reflect my soul
With all of its light and vibrancy
Wanted to emulate my mother
Her green eyes that were destined for the screen
I hid behind my words
And hummed haunted Melodies
I'm older now
My body changed
My face changed
I stayed the same
But no one cared to see
The roaring fire blazing in me
My haunted eyes and kindred soul
All that mattered were the curves under my
jeans
Not the way I think
Or my sequined speak
My poetic heart
Was obsolete
To hungry men

Some of which I thought were Kin
My muddled worlds and static rhymes
Didn't matter before
When I wore more flesh and crooked glasses
I guess it's safe to assume
They wouldn't matter now
Just because I'm desirable enough
to be accepted in a room

Emily Post

You only want to claim my success
Negating the scars you left behind
There for the limelight
Abandoning me in the dark night of the soul
I'm not a porcelain doll demure to flaunt
Not a meal ticket for you to punch when you
feel so inclined
My dreams are my own
I pretend like your acid doesn't burn
Hide the holes with a phosphorus smile
And kind eyes
Laugh unwillingly to hide the pain deep inside
I'm not
Meek and timid
Something small
For you to shape
Into what you see fit
If I'm kind I'm weak
Assertive too abrasive
I'm not a paint by the numbers
I can fill in my own lines
Let me go
My pain is my own
It isn't something you get to define

Release

Am I too haunted?
Embalmed in these moments
Sitting in the shadows
with my ghosts
that you won't let me bury
The wound has been cured
throbbing like a bloated carcass
Flies fighting with the buzzard
Over the rot of muscle
My memories feel infected
throbbing and hot to the touch
I'm afraid to cut them out
Afraid to bleed again
Wondering who I will be
If I detach the rot from my mind no
Afraid the cure will cost too much
I keep picking at the puss
Letting it harden under my nails
Can I create without the cracks?

Sineater

I saw death on a Sunday
It woke me from my dream
We were sitting on the balcony
In a theater
Haunted since god was a child
If you believe in that superstitious stuff
I think way too much
Of old gods and religions hushed
Satanic nightmare
Sweet harmony
Existential daydream
let the gnostics comfort me
Every time I romanticize my Demise
Visualize my brain on the steeple
I think of your blurry eyes
And remember we're not most people
I step back from the ledge
And let you take me home
I met your brother
In the pews
He professed god wasn't coming to save me
I almost believed him too
Maybe is just an illusion
Maybe it's just what we believe
But you've got an edge that cuts
And I've got a lifetime to bleed

Apophis

I chose this
To learn from being still
To find silence in the chaos
That threatened to swallow me like the sun
I yearned for mediocrity
A white picket fence
and folded laundry
But felt stifled
In the chokehold
Of the new Americana
I wanted to fix a house that was torn apart
Mend bloodlines and haunted faces
Dig through records while the world was asleep
Scratch the vinyl and crease the sleeve
Feel the lyrics reverberate through me
Write on ripped pages
And let the ink bleed through
Clutch the words of dead men to my heart
I flirted with domestication
But all I know is art

Ashes

I saw your life flash before my eyes
The demon that you love
That time won't let you bury
I know the blade behind the scar
I felt your essence seep into mine
I know your heart
And I know why it's breaking
There's a little bit less of you every time
You sweep up the ashes in a dust pan
And choke on the embers time has yet to
extinguish
Im jealous of your ghosts
The phantoms swirling in your mind
It's not fair of me
But I wish I didn't have to share you with them
That all of your darkness was mine alone

Compartmentalized

It's been three months
the suitcase is still packed
eagerly awaiting to be deconstructed
torn apart so it can be hollow again
a hard shell in the back of my closet
it stays rutted in the carpet
Immoveable impenetrable
the zipper is sealed watertight
If I open it up, then it's real
admitting the truth while breaking the seal
Littered in clothes from a past life
staring at the wrinkled luggage tag
If I unpack it, then it's true
that wherever I go, I take me too

Love

There's stale venom
You smile
as you cut out the coagulated mass
You took a bite of my heart
to see if it was still beating
It's bitter
and you like the taste
Your shadow still hangs in the corporal of my
vision
Smiling it taunts me
You're just starting to heal
I'm beginning to bleed
There's a swarm of locusts
They tried to make me their home
But I was condemned

Strigoi

I've lived a million lives no one can see
I can't be the roots for a dying tree
sins are mummified in memory
there's too much grey to see
The ground is quaking
I'm dead
But finally breathing
Waking up in a tomb
Inhaling the night
Letting it collect in my chest
Ready to feed off the emptiness
and make a body from the scraps

Hostage

All my dreams end up being sold
Beauty stains
Memories snare
Etched in my skull
Trauma never sleeps
Nether can I
Hostage to my thoughts
There's no exit sign in my brain
I can't find my way out
And I know no one's coming to save me
That role is reserved for me alone
When I'm strong enough to stand
Without my legs buckling
Under the weight
Of my heart
Heavy from all that it holds

Muse

I'm terrified
I'm choking on my heartbeat
Prisoner to primal commands
Subject to a biological conspiracy
Chemicals flushing through my electrodes
I'm smiling at the wall
Illuminated by your memory
Numb to the world around me
Was there something there
or was it just an intrusive thought?
The fire in your eyes that blazed right through
You showed me your teeth
I can't control it the blush in my cheeks
I wish I wasn't as tall
So I could have rested my head on your heart
Was I too vulnerable showing you where I was
cut
You pulled me in closer when I tried to leave
There's blood blistering around my heart
Crusted over and bulging through the surface

Bright

And we exist
Particles of light
Accelerated hearts
Quick to break slow to mend
I'm happy
To know it's okay not to be
And that where I am is where I am supposed to
be
That love is the secret we're all trying to learn
We hear about it in whispers
Through folklore and faded sightings
I've found it everywhere
We choose not to see it
It takes a lifetime to remember
I'm slow to anger and quick to regret
Overthinking my existence
Crippled by my cynicism
I am light even when I can't see it
I am infinite even when I can't feel it
We are eternity in earthly bodies

Desire

I don't want picture perfect memories
Shining and polished
For the world to see
I want you
And your smudged ink
Your faded speak
I want love
Passion
Purpose
To create something worthwhile
A flower in concrete
I want to make art
And feel the paint coated in my soul
Write things that no one will ever read
Or maybe they will
And some of my blood will hold meaning
To a stranger
I'm old fashioned when it comes to love
Nontraditional with everything in between

Shore

I want you
More than I've wanted anything
You're not a toy I can coerce someone into
buying
Not a prize I can win with a flick of my wrist
and a deflated balloon
I want to hold your heart in my hand
Know it's beating for me
Feel your soul entangled in mine
Try to capture the way light flows in your eyes
I want all of you
And I want you
To want every part of me
Yearn for me
Like uncharted land
Foreign and ancient
Waiting for you to realize
The jagged edges are home

Solace

I've made my peace with never finding it
A rose will grow from my corpse
My borrowed flesh will rot in a silk box
Time will fade my name in the stone
My love will stain the sky
Tainting the cosmos
My blood will pollute the veins of strangers
Or maybe it won't
I might be the last of this bloodline
My soul is old
My vessel will catch up
Wrinkled and hollow
In a parking lot full of ghosts

Worth

And she was there
Waiting silently
For me to remember
That child with a heart unsullied
Was still there
In every song
With each tear
In every heartbreak
In every stumble
She echoes in everything I do
She is still waiting
For me to love her
To know she's enough
I'm wearing her around
And I love her
I don't think I did until this moment
but I love her
with every crack
and every scar
She watched me climb out of the pit
She gave me her hand
She carried me to where I am
And I'm enough

www.ingramcontent.com/pod-product-compliance
Lightning Source LLC
LaVergne TN
LVHW010842200726

843508LV00012B/2720